CLOSING THE DOOR, *but not my Heart*

Trenda Lineback

CLOSING THE DOOR, *but not my Heart*

Published by Lineback Books
La Mirada, CA - 2015

SECOND EDITION

Cover and Interior Design:
Cathy Arkle – www.cathyarkle.com

For more information visit:
www.TrendaLineback.com

ISBN: 978-0-692-40638-0

RECOMMENDATIONS

"I just finished reading this book and...WOW! I recommend *Closing the Door, but not my Heart* to all those who have been heart broken over a loved one who has destroyed their connection to family or friends. God brought back Trenda's prodigal son and performed a miracle beyond her expectations...there is nothing too hard for God."

- Ben Read, Pastor of Catholic Rainbow Outreach

"What do you get when you combine the love of a mother and the faithfulness of God? You get a story like Trenda's *Closing the Door, but not my Heart.* Guaranteed to give you a faithlift! It is an inspiring read. Enjoy!"

- Dan Kotoff, Discipleship Pastor, Cottonwood Church

DEDICATION

This book is dedicated, first and foremost, to my Lord and Savior, Jesus Christ. He put all of this together and allowed me to share my story.

I would also like to dedicate this book to my son, Travis, whom I love so very much. Thank you, son, for always loving and believing in me, especially when I had to make some very hard decisions concerning our lives together.

And last, but not least, I want to dedicate this book to my wonderful and loving husband, Ed. Thank you for encouraging me to write this book and for being patient with me. I love you, honey, with all of my heart. You are the best! Thank you for your great love and support.

TABLE *of* CONTENTS

FOREWORD

Closing the Door, But Not My Heart is a powerful story of a young mother who couldn't quit, even when she tried. It's a story of how faith, perseverance and the power of prayer can guide you into your destiny. Trenda Lineback shows what enduring faith looks like. She learned from her mistakes, became a serious seeker of God and connected to a community of believers in a local church that teaches how to live a victorious Christian life.

Having served as Trenda's pastor during the season when she initially gave herself to growing in Jesus, I saw a woman who became bold in her faith and ministered to others with confidence. Her book can serve as a manual for restoration of relationships while keeping God first.

Trenda knows God is faithful and His Word is true. God is not a respecter of persons and He is a rewarder of those who diligently seek Him.

As you read this wonderful book, you will be encouraged that it pays to have hope and faith in the restoration power of God."

To God be the glory!

Pastor Ed Smith
Life Coach, Zoe Christian Fellowship
Whittier, California

ACKNOWLEDGEMENTS

I want to thank all of the people who stood by me through all of this. Those who encouraged me and were there for me truly deserve to be acknowledged. I also want to thank the ones who have invested in my son, Travis, who have made an impact on his life and on my life as well. God used each one of you in a very special and unique way. Thank you for being there for us. Thank you for being obedient to the Lord.

Pastor Ben Read of CRO (Catholic Rainbow Outreach), thank you! From all of us moms, who have been standing and waiting to see our sons return back to God, thank you, Pastor Ben, and your wonderful wife LaVinia. Your ministry is awesome and truly needed. Thank you for being faithful and obedient to our Lord.

Thank you, Pastor Ed Smith of Zoe Christian Fellowship, for teaching us who we are in Christ. Minister Arnold Carter of Zoe Christian Fellowship, thank you for always being there for our family. Special thanks to Minister Shyrea Mills of Zoe Christian Fellowship, my personal mentor and a close friend to all of us. And to Ella Thompson, who trusted the Lord and gave my son a job during his recovery at Catholic Rainbow Outreach – thank you, Ella.

To Pastor Dan Kotoff of Cottonwood Church, thank you especially for being the first one to read my story and for praying for my book. Thank you, Pastor Dan, for your encouragement.

Thank you Pastor Bayless Conley, Senior Pastor of Cottonwood Church, for allowing the Lord to use you the way He does, and thank you for having the ministry of Celebrate Recovery. Truly, it is all about bringing a living Jesus to a dying world.

To Pastor Gene Petrini of Cottonwood Church (Celebrate Recovery), a special thanks for investing in Travis and allowing him to serve in the Celebrate Recovery ministry.

And thank you, Reverend Nick Mangoutas of Cottonwood Leadership College, for being obedient to the Holy Spirit and for the word of confirmation you spoke to me about writing this book.

I especially want to thank Sherry Ward, founder of Square Tree Publishing, and to her entire team, for caring about me and my story. They let me know that my message counts and what I have to say is important. As a new author, I found a very special publisher who believed in me. Sherry and her team could see beyond what I could see. Thank you to Melodie Fox for being so patient with me in all of the content editing. Of course, a big thank you to my special editors, Deborah Chambers and Donna Barrese, for giving me that special one-on-one attention that I so needed. I would like to thank Travis Williams for doing such a good job on formatting my book. Cathy Arkle you did an outstanding job on the front cover, and the interior design as well, thank you so much. God places people in our lives for times and seasons. Thank you God for these wonderful people You have placed in my life. From one new author, I say a big thank you, with more books to come. All glory goes to God.

It took a team of people through the years, a team who kept praying, encouraging me and listening with an open heart, to whom I am forever grateful. If you find yourself in my position of standing in the gap for a loved one who is lost and perhaps rebellious, I encourage you to connect with people you can be honest with and confide in and who you can call on in your times of need. Don't try to carry this all alone. Be willing to be transparent and honest. We are a family in Christ and God will bring these wonderful people across your path to encourage you and lift you up. I am forever grateful to those God brought and continues to bring my way to strengthen me.

INTRODUCTION

This story was written to encourage and help parents and grandparents who have been waiting to see their children set free from all forms of addiction. There is hope through Jesus Christ our Lord! I wanted to share my story of how God set my son totally free from all of his addictions. I spent 14 years standing on God's promises - praying and waiting. I know that nothing, absolutely nothing, is too difficult for our God.

I am just one mom who would like to share her story with you. If you have a son or daughter, or someone you are responsible for, that may have made some bad choices or wrong decisions in their life, perhaps this book can help you.

I certainly do not have all the answers, but I know someone that does. God truly cares for us and for our children. If you allow the Holy Spirit to help you and comfort you, there is victory for you as well as your children.

DON'T GIVE UP

"Thus says the Lord: A voice was heard in Ramah, lamentation and bitter weeping, Rachel weeping for her children, refusing to be comforted for her children, because they are no more." [1] (*Jeremiah 31:15*) I felt like Rachel. My only son was lost in a world

of drugs and alcohol, and I was helpless, unable to save him. How could I feel comfort when I could not reach him? It was a world that I once knew, yet it was the Lord who had rescued me and I had to trust Him to do the same for my son. I was thankful that for now I had a group of people praying for me and for him to be delivered out of the darkness of this time in our lives. These incredible intercessors prayed when I was too tired and sometimes when I just didn't want to pray another prayer. You can get so weary when you are standing in the gap, year after year, when nothing seems to change. Thank God these prayer warriors stood with me on the Word of God!

I stayed in the book of Jeremiah a lot during those years, and I still do today. One Scripture I clung to was, "*Behold, I am the Lord, the God of all flesh. Is there anything too hard for Me?*" [2] (*Jeremiah 32:27*) This Scripture let me take in a deep breath and relax. I knew God would take care of my son and that, in His strength, I could stand no matter what He called me to do. I had to make some very tough decisions during those years. I was standing, waiting for my son to return to God. You may find yourself in this same place. Perhaps you are a parent or grandparent watching your precious loved one being destroyed daily by addictions. You may have tasted the bitter tears that Rachel wept night after night. Don't give up, dear one! My story is here for you to find hope and encouragement, and to find the strength to carry on another day.

"You will hold your child once again in your arms, free from all addictions."

I had carried that boy of mine within me for eight months and had rejoiced at welcoming him into this world. I loved him, cared for him and wanted the very best for him. For most of us, those nine months feel like forever - forever being uncomfortable in your clothes and in your own body. The day finally arrives to produce that baby and the pain can be unbearable. But you didn't give up. Even if you waited for years to adopt your child, you didn't give up. You knew that you would hold that little one in your arms and forget all of your pain. You will hold your child once again in your arms, free from all addictions.

This book is not just about my personal testimony, but about some of the choices I made and how they significantly impacted my son's life. I believe that made a big difference on the choices he made.

Unfortunately, I had experienced addiction in my own life, but nothing like what my son was about to enter into for the next 14 years. Don't give up! It may be that for now you have to close the door to that child, but not your heart.

"Don't give up! It may be that for now you have to close the door to that child, but not your heart."

CHAPTER 1

ROCKY BEGINNINGS

MAY 1966

I was only 17 years old when I first married and didn't know at the time it was the beginning of a life of failed relationships. I was young and in love. It was May of 1966 when we said, "I do." That very next month, June, I graduated from high school. We had just 30 days together before my new husband shipped out with the U.S. Navy and headed for Vietnam. We had known this was going to happen but were determined to get married anyway. After nine months overseas, he returned home to me, and that's when things began to change.

MARCH 1967

Life was tough and my husband struggled to find a job. It was a hard way to start a new life together. My husband experienced a terrible war that no one wanted, while trying to provide for his new bride. I had gotten a job in the aerospace industry and was able to get my husband a job there as well. Whether it was there all along or brought out by the enormous struggles he was going through, a terrible controlling and demanding side of his personality began to emerge. I wanted to be a wife and a mother, but family life was not in my husband's plans. It seemed he was always angry with me or with life in general. It was a natural progression of sorts, and before long, he began to be verbally and physically abusive. Many times I would find myself on the floor, struggling to pick myself up after he had gone off the deep end. I wanted to love and believe in him. I wanted so badly for things to work out. He would always say he was sorry and swear to never hurt me again, but then the nightmare of this life would start over and nothing would change. All I wanted was to be a family. My heart's desire was to be a mother. Like so many others who are in a difficult marriage, I thought things would be different if we started a family. So after three years of waiting, I became pregnant.

AUGUST 1969

I was so excited! I was 20 years old now and I was going to be a mom for the first time. On August 26, 1969, my son Travis Lee Cox was born. He was the joy of my life. I had never been around little babies before and I was a very nervous new mom. He needed a lot of care. He came into this world a month premature and weighed just 4 pounds 12 ounces when he was born. He was delivered in my eighth month of pregnancy. The doctor said it was due to stress. He was so tiny, and that made

"I was so young and now responsible for this fragile little life."

me feel very scared. I was so young and now responsible for this fragile little life.

Love would give me the strength to care for him, and I fell in love with him immediately. So did my parents. They adored him. I know his father loved him, too. He was such a blessing to our whole family.

During that first year of his precious life, Travis became very sick. He had recurring ear infections so severe they caused him to be in constant pain. He needed me to be there for him for everything. I wanted to be such a good mother. My life would revolve around the times Travis needed this medicine, which could be any time of the day or night. This often caused conflict between my husband and me. My troubled and stressful marriage wasn't getting any better, and my devotion to Travis only seemed to add to it all. I wanted to be a stay-at-home mom, and my husband wanted me to go back to work. He made it clear to me many times that his paycheck alone would not be enough. When Travis was just three months old, reluctantly, I went back to work.

Going back to work full-time did not solve our marriage problems. It wasn't long before my husband would spend more and more time away from our new family. He planned vacations without me and was gone on fishing trips most of the time. It seemed as if he wanted to live like a single man, yet remain married to me as well. Divorce was not an option with him, and he had made that very clear to me. Once, to make a point, he went into the other room and he loaded a Colt 45 revolver. I could hear him sliding the rounds into the cylinder one at a time. Next I heard him spin the cylinder as he closed it up. Then he came back into the room where I was. He pulled back the hammer on the gun and aimed it at my head and then at his own head. Then he just turned and walked away. I knew he didn't want to talk divorce anymore.

FREEDOM, 1972

Although it seemed impossible, after six and a half years together, I finally walked out of our marriage and filed for divorce. I had also found out that my husband had been unfaithful to me while we were married. He tried hard to fight the divorce. I was the only one keeping the marriage together, and I was so tired of trying to do it all by myself. When Travis was just three years old, my dysfunctional marriage was over. However, a foundation was laid for my son, seeds of rejection and heartache that, little did I know, would take root and grow into a great battle for us both to face. I wish I had seen a glimpse of the rejection then, but I had let those same seeds sprout in me. They led me to failed relationship after relationship and into my own addictions. I was blinded by my own pain at times, but God was not in the dark over my situation. He had a hope and future for both of us, even back then, though I didn't even know He existed.

"God had a hope and future for us both, even back then, though I didn't even know He existed."

NOTES/PRAYERS FOR LOVED ONES

Behold, I am the Lord, the God of all flesh. Is there anything too hard for Me?
Jeremiah 32:27

CHAPTER 2

SEEDS OF REJECTION

In the same year that I got divorced, I got married again. The clerk didn't bat an eye when I picked up my divorce papers at one window of city hall and then my new marriage license at another. Fearful of abuse from my first marriage, I was determined to NEVER find myself in a situation like that again. This new marriage lasted only one year. I felt the rejection of another failed marriage and divorce. I wanted Travis to have a family like the other kids he knew, with a mom and a dad. Disappointment set in as I was back to being a single mother, just Travis and me. This was hard on me but must have been just as hard on my son.

It was about this time that Travis's dad moved up north, and the distance made it difficult for him to visit with Travis. He had remarried as well, yet Travis was still his only child. I wanted them to be close, in spite of the distance, but the visits were few. From the time Travis was four years old up until he became a teenager, I would put him on a plane almost every summer to visit his dad. Just like all boys, he wanted to spend some one-on-one time with his father, but that rarely seemed to happen. I tried to fill that empty spot, but I just couldn't do it. Rejection had set in for my son, and this was so hard on him while growing up. Rejection is one of the toughest issues to deal with, no matter what your age. Travis and I have had many conversations about how he felt back then. I thought I was to blame for so many of his bad choices, but he told me many times how angry and hurt he felt over being rejected by his father. I still felt guilty. I had made many bad choices, all while Travis was there watching.

"I still felt guilty. I had made many bad choices, all while Travis was there watching."

BAD EXAMPLE

I know Travis was watching me very closely, and by this time I sure wasn't setting a good example for him to follow. My lifestyle had become so different by now. I had turned to alcohol and prescription drugs to numb my brokenness and the deep pain I felt. I had also, unexpectedly, found myself a victim of sexual abuse. Someone I had trusted had violated that trust and threw my world into chaos and confusion. This horror only added more pain in my life. I felt like a complete failure. Travis had to go through all this with me. I would ask him to bring my wine and pills to me. He was so young and innocent, and I would tell him, "Bring mom her pills". I remember this so well, and unfortunately, Travis does

"You don't often see the way things really look when you are filled with hurt that goes deep down into your soul."

too. You don't often see the way things really look when you are filled with hurt that goes deep down into your soul.

A DOWNWARD SPIRAL

I became addicted to alcohol and prescription medicine. I jumped from relationship to relationship, dating men with no commitment from either of us. This was so damaging to my son. There was no one for Travis to look up to except his grandfather. My dad set a great example for him, but I wasn't doing such a great job as a mom. We had to move several times as well, and this meant changing schools. Travis attended several different elementary schools and became a regular in the after-school program. My mother would watch him for me as often as she could, but I was forced to work two jobs to support us. I remembered how I was there for him constantly when he was a baby, and now it seemed like I wasn't there at all. Why was life so messed up for us? And all the while, dark feelings haunted me. Wine and pills barely kept the pain at arm's length from all I had been through.

There is a Scripture that tells about how God could find no one to stand in the gap for mankind, to save him from all his sins, and so He stood in the gap for us Himself. I did not realize at the time that one day I would know that feeling of standing for someone who could not stand for himself, my own precious son. I didn't know then that God was standing in the gap for me. "*He saw that there was no man, and wondered that there was no intercessor; therefore His own arm brought salvation for Him; and His own righteousness, it sustained Him."* [1] *(Isaiah 59:16)*

I was living on the edge of destruction, clinging to a life that would not hold together long. Something was about to give, and my precious Savior, so unknown to me, but so very kind and tender, was standing, praying, holding onto me while I wrestled with not wanting to go on any longer. What happened in my life next was truly a miracle.

NOTES/PRAYERS FOR LOVED ONES

Behold, I am the Lord, the God of all flesh. Is there anything too hard for Me?
Jeremiah 32:27

CHAPTER 3

JESUS, ARE YOU REAL?

NOVEMBER 1979

In November of 1979, alcohol and pills could no longer numb the pain. I didn't want to live anymore. I had convinced myself that everyone would be better off without me. I knew my parents would raise Travis and take good care of him if I were gone. He was my main concern. I believed that my life would no longer be a burden to anyone. No one would have to worry about me if I were dead. I just wanted the pain to stop. I was only thinking of myself at the time. I had tried to end my life once before by taking pills, but it hadn't worked. However, this time I was going to make sure it worked. Jesus said, "*The thief does not come except to steal, and to kill, and to destroy. I have come that they may have life, and that they may have it more abundantly.*" [1] (*John 10:10*) I had no idea

> **"As I began to swing my arm towards the mirror to break the glass, something or someone blocked my hand and pushed me back. I saw and heard no one."**

at the time that it was Satan who was the thief trying to steal my life and all that I held close. At 31 years old, most people are just beginning to reach their stride and enjoy life. I was too tired of the pain to continue mine. I had it all carefully planned out, or so I thought. I had locked the door to my bedroom and went into the connecting bathroom. I was going to break the glass mirror and cut my throat with a jagged edge. I gathered my nerve and made a fist. As I began to swing my arm towards the mirror to break the glass, something or someone blocked my hand and pushed me back. I found myself on the floor. I closed my eyes tight as the room began to spin. Suddenly, I saw all these men's faces that had hurt me so badly. They were surrounding me. They were spinning around and around and around. It felt like a Twlight Zone episode.

I was at a loss at what to do now. I found myself crying out in a loud voice, "Jesus! Jesus, if you are real, prove it to me". I was a like a crazy person, on the floor, shaking all over, screaming. Incredibly, I heard a voice say to me, "Trenda, I love you". At that moment, I just broke down. I was completely undone. I felt these arms around me just holding me and this incredible warmth that covered me from my head to my feet. I sat on the floor and began to weep. It was as if I had been in darkness for all those years, and then suddenly someone came and turned the light on in me. Here I was, sitting on the floor crying, and Jesus was holding me and rocking me. It was an indescribable feeling. I had felt so rejected for so long. And now God loved me for me. I didn't have to pretend anymore. I truly had a "road to Damascus salvation" and I have never been the same since. I became born again that day, and I knew from that point on, nothing was too hard for God, absolutely nothing. He had proven it to me on that lonely day in November 1979. For "*whoever calls on the name of the Lord shall be saved.*" [2] (*Romans 10:13*)

DECEMBER 1979

My son was nine years old when Jesus reached out and saved me. Travis quickly received Jesus also. He began to lead his friends to the Lord. He truly loved God and our lives really changed. I was radically saved and was not looking back. My son watched his mom change right before his very eyes. I was no longer the same. I wanted to live for Jesus. We stopped moving from place to place and finally settled into a home where we lived for the next 15 years. I was not the same mom Travis had known his whole life. I was so happy, and he was so happy too. This life was still so very new to us and we both had to grow up together. We started going to a small Southern Baptist church. God had used my son to get us there. We could walk to it from our house. God had it all worked out. We were planted there for nearly seven and a half years. We became completely involved in that church.

"My son watched his mom change right before his very eyes. I was no longer the same."

After a few years, I became a youth director there and Travis was involved with the youth group. This was an exciting and great new challenge for me. My son was about 13 years old at the time. We had some very hard core teenagers at our church and we didn't want to discourage them from coming. God loved them too. I began to share my testimony, letting people know that nothing – absolutely nothing – is ever too hard for our Lord and Savior. I was involved with our Skid Row ministry, rehab homes for women, and everything I could get involved in when those church doors opened. My life had changed from night to day. It seemed like everything was finally going great for us.

DOING TOO MUCH

It was now 1984 and I was involved with the music ministry, leading teams in a homeless ministry, singing, and teaching the youth. I had more meetings to attend and more demands on my time. I was also working a full-time job at a major aerospace company and was required to work a lot of overtime when there were deadlines to meet. As a result, Travis was often home alone.

My plate had too many things on it. In fact, it was overflowing! I was on fire for the Lord and wanted to express it in the only way I knew how, by serving. I thought I was doing the right thing, but I still had a teenager at home who needed me. He was alone at home so much of the time while I was at church.

> **" Our family is our ministry too. Serving them is serving God as well."**

I am not trying to discourage anyone from serving the Lord in any way, but I encourage you to do that one thing you know you are called to do. God will open the doors when the time is right.

Remember, our family is our ministry too. Serving them is serving God as well. I remember what a pastor once told me. He said, "Trenda, find that one place where you know you should be. Serve in that one place with all your heart. In that way, you can serve with excellence." So that's what I began to do. I felt called to lead people to salvation and into the baptism of the Holy Spirit. That has been my calling from the very beginning.

SUBTLE CHANGES

Travis was reaching that age where boys begin to change physically as well as in every other area. He was about 14 years old at the time. Someone had given me a book to read called "How to Really Love Your Teenager", but I would soon find out that I needed much more help than that. I had never raised a teenager before, and to tell the truth, I was growing up myself in this new life with Jesus and may have been quite blinded to what my son needed at the time. I began to see changes in him, subtle changes, but never realized they were signs of the pain and heartache that we were about to face.

NOTES/PRAYERS FOR LOVED ONES

Behold, I am the Lord, the God of all flesh. Is there anything too hard for Me?
Jeremiah 32:27

CHAPTER 4

TROUBLING CHANGES

I started to notice that my son, and some of the kids he hung around with from church, began acting strange. I couldn't quite put my finger on it, but they seemed different somehow. Travis and I began to have a hard time communicating. We struggled to understand one another. We had more arguments than ever before. He became so rebellious towards me. Even his teachers at school began to notice the changes in his behavior.

I had no idea what was beginning to happen. Neither did I know what signs to look for. I was radically saved and I thought Travis had wanted this new life also. Looking back, I can see that all those long nights that he was by himself had left room for my son to be deceived and lured into the entrapments of the enemy. While I was at church serving, my son was at home alone. Although he was interested in music, he still had a lot of idle time on his hands. We had neighbors who were alcoholics, and my son and their son were friends. I had no idea Travis had begun drinking at the age of 12. I can't believe I didn't see it. His attitude was getting really bad. I was so naïve. I thought he was just being a normal teenager.

PRAYER WARRIORS NEEDED

I needed help. I was in a church that didn't teach very much or very often on the authority we have over the devil. I had no idea how to stand and fight for what belongs to me as a child of God. I didn't know my rights as a Christian. I started asking people to pray for my son. I sought the Scriptures for answers, and I found out that our helper is the Holy Spirit. I had no idea how to tap into this power, but I knew I needed His help. "*But you shall receive power when the Holy Spirit has come upon you, and you shall be witnesses to Me in Jerusalem, and in all Judea and Samaria, and to the end of the earth.*"[1] (*Acts 1:8*)

NEW INFLUENCES

The familiar faces that I once saw surrounding my son began to change. A different set of friends soon circled him at school. His grades started dropping dramtically. Up to this point, Travis was a very good student with good grades. He was very smart. I thought learning to drive might help our relationship and his attitude towards me and towards school. He applied for his driver's permit when he turned 15 1/2 years old, and as soon as he turned 16 years old, he applied for his driver's license. He passed all of his tests and was on his way to independence. Sometimes I let him use my car. I wanted to be a great mom.

FIRST JOB, FIRST PHONE CALL

In order to help pay for the car insurance and to teach him a little responsibility, I made Travis get a job. He worked for a large retail store that was close to home and he could walk to work. Of course this didn't happen very often, not with a teenager who has his own driver's license. Travis had been working there for a few months when I received a devastating phone call. Travis had been discovered stealing food. I was totally shocked! They said they had been watching him for awhile. I was dumbfounded. I asked, "Are you sure? Not my son! I feed him." I couldn't understand why this was happening. I spoke with the store manager about the situation. Thank God they did not turn Travis in to the authorities over this one, but it was such an embarrassment to us all. This was such a blow, losing his first job at age 16 in this way.

After this incident, I thought something like this would never happen again. However, this was just the beginning of a long and painful journey for us both. Something was really missing from Travis' life. I know not all kids act out to the degree my son did. Travis had no father at home, and the father he did have seemed to find no time for him. This had left such a void in Travis, a void he was trying to fill. I wasn't sure how to reach Travis myself. He was making big choices that were altering the course of his life, and I struggled to help him get back on track.

HELP FROM THE HOLY SPIRIT

I didn't know about the baptism of the Holy Spirit for almost six and a half years into my Christian life. I had no idea that He is my helper and comforter and teacher. In 1985, I received the baptism of the Holy Spirit through my wonderful friend Shyrea. She became my mentor and close friend, which she still is to this day. She explained to me that the baptism of the Holy Spirit was a whole new way of talking to the Lord. Praying in other tongues was the help I needed. I would get so tired of praying in English about the same old thing. I needed a new approach; I wanted to see some results.

I never realized that you can confuse the devil with your prayer language. Satan can't interrupt God's Spirit because the Holy Spirit is the Spirit of truth. I knew this type of praying was for me! "*And I will pray the Father, and He will give you another Helper, that He may abide with you forever – the Spirit of truth whom the world cannot receive, because it neither sees Him nor knows Him; but you know Him, for He dwells with you and will be in you.*" [2] (*John 14:16-17*) The devil had confused me long enough. The Holy Spirit prays for those things that we don't know how to pray for. "*Likewise the Spirit also helps in our weaknesses. For we do not know what we should pray for as we ought, but the Spirit Himself makes intercession for us with groanings which cannot be uttered.*" [3] (*Romans 8:26*)

"I never realized that you can confuse the devil with your prayer language."

THINGS GREW WORSE

Things started coming up missing in my home, items that I knew were not misplaced. Then I began to find drug paraphernalia. I confronted Travis, but his answer was always the standard, "It's not mine, it belongs to my friend". I would then tell him, "Okay, then change friends". You always want to give your son or daughter the benefit of the doubt. I wanted to believe that my son wasn't involved in such things. Maybe I was too naïve as a single parent.

"I will bless those who bless you, And I will curse him who curses you; And in you all the families of the earth shall be blessed." [4] (*Genesis 12:3*) God's original plan for families was to consist of a father, a mother, and children. Unfortunately some of us have to be single parents, some by choice and some having no other choice.

MY HEART IS BROKEN

It broke my heart to know that my only son was turning away from the Lord and turning to a lifestyle of addiction. I really didn't know what to do. Ever since he was nine years old, he loved going to church and he truly loved the Lord. Now he was a teenager, and life had become completely different. I was a single mom raising an only child, a challenge for anyone.

I found out Travis was smoking marijuana. I was so hurt. I had been delivered from wine and valium, and neither drugs nor alcohol was allowed in my home. At this time, I was still struggling with smoking cigarettes myself. I knew I wasn't setting a good example, but it didn't justify allowing drugs or alcohol in my home. I had been delivered, and there was no way I would allow this to happen again. I contacted Victory Outreach Ministries. They told me they had a teen program located out in the California desert. I approached Travis with this idea and his response was, "NO WAY! You're not sending me to the desert." He promised me that there would be no more drugs. He was done with them. He said it in such a way that I believed him and took him at his word. I think I blamed myself for why all of this was happening to my son. I felt guilty for leaving him alone all those nights and for being a bad example early on with my own addictions. I felt like a failure to my son. I thought I was not a good mom and that all of this was my fault. Suddenly, I remembered what God's Word says: "*The thief does not come except to steal, and to kill, and to destroy. I have come that they may have life, and that they may have it more abundantly.*" [5] (*John 10:10*) Satan is the enemy and he will attack us where it hurts us the most. He wants to destroy the things we love and care about. For me, of course, this was my son.

CHURCH CHANGES

Our wonderful little church was not meeting all of our spiritual needs. By now I had already received the baptism of the Holy Spirit. I was praying in other tongues, and tapping into this wonderful new amazing power that our Lord Jesus had promised us. I found out the Holy Spirit is my helper and comforter. And I needed all the extra help I could get. I also needed agreement. It appeared that our little church was not open to the baptism of the Holy Spirit. I did not want to cause any confusion, but I knew I needed to make a change. I needed help and I needed to know how to fight the devil. Demons are real, and I needed all the help I could get. So I began my search to find a church that fit that bill.

I found a church in Downey that believed in the baptism of the Holy Spirit. I started going to this new church around 1988. I attended there for a few years, and it was a good start for me. As time went on, I knew I needed more help with my son. I needed true prayer warriors to be on my side. I say warriors because we are in a battle; we have to fight for our children. Be careful who you ask to pray for your children. Make sure they truly believe that nothing is too hard for God. It is so important to know the authority we have as believers in Christ. I needed help and hope to get through this. God knew there were many tough years ahead of me. I had no idea it was going to be a long 14 years, but God did, and He knew where to send me. I had to stand on God's promises and keep on standing. This wonderful Scripture gave me the strength to do just that: "*Wherefore take unto you the whole armour of God, that ye may be able to withstand in the evil day, and having done all, to stand.*" [6] (*Ephesians 6:13 KJV*)

JUNE 1988

On June 4, 1988, I smoked my last cigarette. I started attending a Christian drug program at Crenshaw Christian Center in Los Angeles. I attended every Thursday night for one year. I felt the Lord had directed me to go there. The Lord gets all the glory for setting me free from this addiction. I had smoked since I was 13 years old, so this was another miracle. This was harder than all of the other addictions I had dealt with in my past. But with God I knew nothing was impossible. But Jesus looked at them and said to them, "*With men this is impossible, but with God all things are possible.*" [7] (*Matthew 19:26*) I knew God could not lie. I wanted to glorify God, inside and out.

So I made a decision. Just because my son was not right with God at this time, I was not going to let this stop me from moving forward with the Lord. I wanted to glorify God, inside and out. I wanted to be totally delivered from all those weights that could keep me from moving forward. I had to stand strong on this because Satan wanted me to cave in and give up. '*Therefore we also, since we are surrounded by so great a cloud of witnesses, let us lay aside every weight, and the sin which so easily ensnares us, and let us run with endurance the race that is set before us.*" [8] *(Hebrews 12:1)*

TROUBLE WITH THE LAW

I received a phone call from the sheriff's station one day saying my son had been arrested for possession of a controlled substance. I had no idea what this man was talking about and replied, "What's that?" His answer to me was, "It's cocaine, lady". My dad had bailed him out. This was the beginning of many calls.

I remember the very first time I went to court for Travis. It was so difficult. I made it a point to always be there for him, supporting him, but I would never bail him out of jail. I had to stand strong on this decision. Once, I was so upset with him that I decided not to show up at court. Travis was looking for me that day. It was heart wrenching to see my son coming through those court doors being chained with other men, all wearing the same jail clothes. All I could do is look at him and cry. Communicating with my child through a glass barrier and using a telephone to talk, when he was so close to me, was a very difficult thing to do. It was overwhelming to realize that one person, a judge, held the power to what would happen to my child, to direct the course of his life without any say from me. That's why we, as parents, need to pray and stand on God's Word for our children's outcome. My father would regularly bail Travis out, and every time he did this, it would lead to a huge conflict between us. This was only hurting Travis, not helping him, and it was always very hard on us all as a family.

"As parents, we need to pray and stand on God's Word for our children's outcomes."

NOTES/PRAYERS FOR LOVED ONES

Behold, I am the Lord, the God of all flesh. Is there anything too hard for Me?
Jeremiah 32:27

CHAPTER 5

THE HARDEST THING

Travis was now 19 years old, and things began to spiral out of control. The fighting between us got worse, there were holes in the walls, and more and more things came up missing. By now Travis could sign my name better than I could on my checks, in order to keep his lifestyle going. Something had to change, and there was only one place this was all leading.

I can still hear his voice through the door as I closed it, 'Mom! Mom! Mom, don't do this to me! Please let me in. You can't just throw me out into the street!" I had put his things in a large plastic bag, his shirts on hangers, and placed some money in an envelope. I made sure he had no house key.

CLOSING THE DOOR FOR THE FIRST TIME

I shut the door, fell on my knees and cried out to God for strength. I can't remember how long I cried, and I wasn't sure where Travis would go. My parents had opened their door to him and that made things continuously worse. Although they didn't know it, they were enabling him. They told me that I really didn't love my son and that I was a horrible mother. Even my best friend said, "How could you do that to him?" I asked her, "Do you want him to live with you?"

"They told me that I really didn't love my son and that I was a horrible mother."

Of course I knew she didn't. I knew God's Word was true and that He would come through for me and our family. I wanted my son to know that God would be there for him too, and that He really did love him. Travis needed to depend on God completely. My heart was broken for my son, and my tears fell often. Travis continued using his drugs and things continued to get worse.

GREAT CONFLICT

My parents and I regularly argued over Travis. They didn't think I should be so upset every time they bailed him out of jail. On at least two occasions, they put their house up as collateral for the bail. I told my son if he didn't show up for court they would lose everything. Through all of this, my parents still thought they were helping their grandson. I was now praying all the time and leaned heavily on my prayer partners. I was keeping my intercessors very busy! They were so very precious and invaluable to me.

LOS ANGELES COUNTY JAIL

I remember my first visit to see my son in jail. I had to be searched. This was an experience all by itself. I had no idea what to expect. I knew Travis wanted to see me, and of course I wanted to see him. He asked me to get him out. It pained me so, but I had to say, "Sorry son, I can't do that". I had to stand strong and use tough love, but this really tore me up inside. Deep down, I knew it was the right thing to do.

Being a mom, you just know when something is not right with your children. One evening, I woke up in the middle of the night and began praying in the spirit for a long time, not sure what was going on. The next day, Travis called me and told me what had happened in his cell at the same time I was praying for him the night before. Some gang members started to come in to his cell, and then all of a sudden, they just left. That was the power of the Holy Spirit at work! I continued praying that Travis would never be violated in any way. God is so good. Nothing did happen to him, and the following day he was transferred to another facility called Wayside.

MY VISIT TO WAYSIDE

I remember this visit so well. I took Jenny, Travis' cousin, with me. Wayside is located in Castaic, California, at the end of an old road that was rightly-named 'Old Road'. I remember driving towards Magic Mountain amusement park and then up a hill where we parked the car and climbed into a minibus filled with people. We continued up the 'Old Road' to Wayside. I really didn't know what to expect. Some of the people on the bus looked just like me, a mother of a troubled child, while others looked lost and confused. Everyone on this bus needed prayer.

It seemed like it took forever to get to the top of the hill. When we finally arrived, I was able to see and talk to Travis through a fence that looked like it was made of chicken wire. What a strange feeling it was to see my son behind this fence. We were allowed to sit on long picnic benches, but this was not a picnic for any of us, that was for sure. The one hour visit seemed so very short. When it was over and we began the long drive back towards Los Angeles, I cried all the way home. I knew Jesus was with me, and Jenny was in the car with me, but I still felt alone. I felt like a failure as a mom.

"I felt like a failure as a mom."

OPENED THE DOOR AGAIN

When Travis was released from Wayside, I said he could move back in with me. He was about 23 years old by this time. But in just a couple of months, he was back to his old ways. He hadn't reached the end of himself yet. So once again, I had to close the door, but not my heart. A new demon called crystal meth had now made its way into Travis' life. I don't remember when he started using this terrible drug, but it really had a grip on him. He was soon arrested again, this time for buying and selling drugs. The arrests now seemed to come more often, and I was starting to get tired of it all.

NOTES/PRAYERS FOR LOVED ONES

Behold, I am the Lord, the God of all flesh. Is there anything too hard for Me?
Jeremiah 32:27

O virgin of Israel!
You shall again be adorned with your [b]tambourines,
And shall go forth in the dances of those who rejoice.

5 [a]You shall yet plant vines on the mountains of Samaria;
The planters shall plant and [1]eat *them* as ordinary food.

6 For there shall be a day
When the watchmen will cry on Mount Ephraim,
[a]'Arise, and let us go up *to* Zion,
To the LORD our God.' "

7 For thus says the LORD:

[a]"Sing with gladness for Jacob,
And shout among the chief of the nations;
Proclaim, give praise, and say,
'O LORD, save Your people,
The remnant of Israel!'

8 Behold, I will bring them [a]from the north country,
And [b]gather them from the ends of the earth,
Among them the blind and the lame,
The woman with child
And the one who labors with child, together;
A great throng shall return there.

9 [a]They shall come with weeping,
And with supplications I will lead them.
I will cause them to walk [b]by the rivers of waters,
In a *straight way in which they shall not stumble;
For I am a *Father to Israel,
And Ephraim *is* My [c]firstborn.

10 "Hear the word of the LORD, O nations,
And declare *it* in the [1]isles afar off, and say,
'He who scattered Israel [a]will gather him,
And keep him as a shepherd *does* his flock.'

11 For [a]the LORD has redeemed Jacob,
And ransomed him [b]from the hand of one stronger than he.

4 [b]Ex. 15:20; Judg. 11:34; Ps. 149:3
5 [a]Ps. 107:37; Is. 65:21; Ezek. 28:26; Amos 9:14 [1]Lit. *treat them as common*
6 [a][Is. 2:3; Jer. 31:12; 50:4, 5; Mic. 4:2]
7 [a]Is. 12:5, 6
8 [a]Jer. 3:12, 18; 23:8 [b]Deut. 30:4; Is. 43:6; Ezek. 20:34, 41; 34:13
9 [a][Ps. 126:5; Jer. 50:4] [b]Is. 35:8; 43:19; 49:10, 11 [c]Ex. 4:22
*See WW at Prov. 3:6. • See WW at Ps. 68:5.
10 [a]Is. 40:11; Ezek. 34:12–14 [1]Or *coastlands*
11 [a]Is. 44:23; 48:20; Jer. 15:21; 50:19 [b]Is. 49:24
12 [a]Ezek. 17:23 [b]Hos. 3:5 [c]Is. 58:11 [d]Is. 35:10; 65:19; [John 16:22; Rev. 21:4]
13 *See WW at Ps. 23:4.
14 [1]Fill to the full *See WW at Amos 4:8.
15 [a]Matt. 2:17, 18 [b]Josh. 18:25; Judg. 4:5; Is. 10:29; Jer. 40:1 [c]Gen. 37:35 [d]Jer. 10:20
16 [a][Is. 25:8; 30:19]
17 [a]Jer. 29:11 *See WW at Hos. 2:15.

12 Therefore they shall come and sing in [a]the height of Zion,
Streaming to [b]the goodness of the LORD—
For wheat and new wine and oil,
For the young of the flock and the herd;
Their souls shall be like a [c]well-watered garden,
[d]And they shall sorrow no more at all.

13 "Then shall the virgin rejoice in the dance,
And the young men and the old, together;
For I will turn their mourning to joy,
Will *comfort them,
And make them rejoice rather than sorrow.

14 I will [1]satiate the soul of the priests with abundance,
And My people shall be *satisfied with My goodness, says the LORD."

Mercy on Ephraim

TRAVIS, WILL RETURN TO GOD 100%

15 Thus says the LORD:

5-29-87

[a]"A voice was heard in [b]Ramah,
Lamentation *and* bitter [c]weeping,
Rachel weeping for her children,
Refusing to be comforted for her children,
Because [d]they *are* no more."

16 Thus says the LORD:

"Refrain your voice from [a]weeping,
And your eyes from tears;
For your work shall be rewarded, says the LORD,
And they shall come back from the land of the enemy.

17 There is [a]hope* in your future, says the LORD,
That your children shall come back to their own border.

18 "I have surely heard Ephraim bemoaning himself:

31:6 Let us go up to Zion: From the time of Jeroboam the people in the northern kingdom worshiped at rival shrines; now they will return to the one place God set His name.
31:15–22 Rachel, mother of Joseph and Benjamin (see Gen. 30:22–24; 35:16–20), laments for her children (the northern tribes who are going into exile, 722 B.C.). V. 15 is quoted in Matt. 2:18 to express grief over the slaughter of innocent babies, but here it introduces the hope of restoration and joy.
31:18–21 The first step in repentance for **Ephraim** (a synonym for Israel) is confession and a **turning** to God (see 3:22–25; Hos. 6:1–3). To prevent a return to the old ways, Ephraim is encouraged to **set up signposts** (31:21) and remember the way that led to punishment.

Wil
ATHLET

CHAPTER 6

A TURN FOR THE WORSE

Travis was at my mother's house when he received the sad news that his dad had passed away at the age of 47. Travis' father was a diabetic who smoked for years and had a history of alcohol abuse. While walking into work one day, he died suddenly. He never knew that his only son was headed down a road of destruction. We kept all of this from him because Travis wanted it that way. This was a tough time for all of us, but it was a terrible loss to Travis.

"I suggested to Travis that it might make him feel better if he wrote his dad a letter and placed it inside the casket."

Travis never did get to tell his dad how he really felt inside, how angry he had been, not having his dad around and part of his life. Yet he loved his dad and wanted to tell him so. My son felt so conflicted. I was still there for him and would always be there for him.

My parents and I went along with Travis and drove up north for the funeral service. I suggested to Travis that it might make him feel better if he wrote his dad a letter and placed it inside the casket. So he wrote a long letter and did just that. I believe it did help a little, yet Travis would still battle anger issues over his dad for many years to come. These issues triggered him to go deeper into the drug life. I hadn't understood the impact of not having a father in the house until my son started acting out his issues through drug use and crime. He had so much anger built up in him, and it was still far from being resolved.

A SERIOUS TURN, GEORGIA 1993

In 1993, Travis and one of his friends left California to visit Georgia. I don't know how long he was there, but it didn't seem that long before he was back in California again. One afternoon while I was at my mother's house, two police officers came to the door. They were looking for my son and wanted to know if I knew where he was. I told them I didn't know where he was, but I was expecting to see him later that night. They told me he comitted a crime in a small town in the state of Georgia in which guns were involved. This was the most serious crime he had been involved in, up to this time. The warrant said Travis was armed. When a warrant reads armed, this means guns are involved. The officers didn't know if Travis was armed or not. One officer told me that my son's life was on the line, and if I truly wanted to help him, I needed to call them and let them know when he got to the house. I told them I would call them because I didn't want my son to lose his life. When Travis arrived, I had my mother take him into another room to talk with him so I could make the phone call without him knowing. My heart was racing on the inside, and I felt like crying. I had to stand strong. I had to stay as calm as possible until the police arrived or my son might get suspicious and try to run. No mother should ever have to make this choice, to call the police on her son, but this was another hard decision I had to make. My son had no idea that I was the one who called the police that night, and he didn't find out for a long time.

Travis was arrested and taken back to the state of Georgia where he committed the crime. What another nightmare this was for us! We were not sure of the outcome, but we were informed he was looking at time in federal prison due to his crime and for fleeing the state.

Travis was held in jail in a very small town in Georgia. Unlike the jails in California where the inmates are supplied with most everything they need, here they didn't even get a tooth brush. I made up a care package for him. I sent him everything he needed. He would call me collect regularly, three or four times a week. He would tell me the sheriff's wife would bring home-cooked food to eat. I thought he was getting off a little easy on this one. Maybe things in this jail weren't that tough after all.

The bail was set and my dad paid it. My dad never did tell me how much he paid. Travis was sent back to us in California. Of course my son wasn't quite done with his rebellious lifestyle just yet. In fact, things only got worse. There were more drugs, but Travis had learned to avoid the police, or so he thought. I constantly kept him covered in prayer. I prayed for his protection and that he would never be violated at any time, in or out of jail. This seemed impossible, knowing the horrors that happen in prisons and jails, but nothing is too hard for God.

"But one thing I knew - God was able to turn all of this around and glorify Himself."

Tensions were running high for all of us at this time, and the circumstances painted a bleak picture. I wasn't sure how all of this was going to turn out. But one thing I knew God was able to turn all of this around and glorify Himself.

NOTES/PRAYERS FOR LOVED ONES

Behold, I am the Lord, the God of all flesh. Is there anything too hard for Me?
Jeremiah 32:27

CHAPTER 7

GROWING WEARY

Many years went by and I saw no change. I was so tired of praying and seeing no real change in my son's situation. One day, I just didn't want to pray for Travis anymore. I told my friend Shyrea that I was done; I wasn't going to pray for my Travis any longer. My flesh was just tired. Perhaps you may have felt this way at some point when you have stood and stood on the Word, and it seems as if nothing is happening. I knew God understood, but this wasn't His plan. God is so good! He brings friends to us, like when Moses' arms grew weary during the battle, to help hold our hands up and strengthen us. Shyrea said she would take over praying for Travis. I said, "Great, for how long?" She laughed and said, "For a little while...you need a break." This was a true friend. Sometimes you just need someone you can count on to step in for you when you need to regroup and rest.

The Lord reminded me not to close my heart on Travis. God never closes His heart to us. I thank God He never gave up on me when I was so lost and out of control. I couldn't give up on my son now. I had to keep going. After a few weeks of Shyrea's help standing in for me, I was encouraged and back on track. My friend gave me the break I needed, so without any guilt, I was now able to continue on with this journey. "*I can do all things through Christ who strengthens me.*" [1] (*Philippians 4:13*) I love this verse! And now with His power working in me, I could do this; I could stand on His Word.

BEING IN A WORD CHURCH

I can't emphasize enough the importance of attending a church that teaches the uncompromised Word of God. Understanding the Scriptures and how they apply to everyday life really does transform the way we think, talk, act and pray.

The Lord used my wonderful friend Shyrea, once again, to lead me to a church that taught the Word so strongly. I began attending Zoe Christian Fellowship with Pastor Ed Smith. The church was meeting at a high school in the city of Cerritos at the time. Pastor Ed was teaching on our identity in Christ and how to take back what Christ bought for us with His blood and what belongs to us as believers. I really needed to hear that.

After five years, we outgrew the school we met in and our church moved to Whittier. This was a great move for us, and we could see that God had a purpose in it. I had no idea where God was going with this, but He did. I just continued standing and praying and believing. All I knew was I wanted my son set free.

I was so happy to be in such a good Bible-teaching church. Pastor Ed always taught us the uncompromising Word of God. His teachings were so clear and easy to understand. It strengthened my belief that nothing was impossible for God. Pastor Ed and his wife Vanessa set a good example of how God wants to bless us and our families. This was the hope I needed for me and Travis. I needed to be around strong uncompromising Christians. They lifted me up and showed me what God can do if we just trust Him.

TRENDA'S CLEANING SERVICE

Pastor Ed had a heart for business and was teaching an entrepreneur course which I began attending. This changed my life. I was already in the beginning stages of starting my own business, but I didn't know what to do or how to run it. This course gave me the tools and the confidence I needed. Trenda's Cleaning Service was off and running. God brought business to me from my home church, and I was able to hire people who needed a job. God supplied all my needs and the needs of others as well. What a blessing it is that I can say that I still run this business today after 25 years! God gets all the glory and honor.

HIGHS AND LOWS

During this amazing time of being a part of a wonderful church and starting a business of my own, Travis was still living in his drug-controlled world. It was easy for discouragement to set in. I stayed in the Word a lot to keep myself encouraged. Sometimes you just have to encourage yourself. King David had to do this as well. "*Now David was greatly distressed, for the people spoke of stoning him, because the soul of all the people was grieved, every man for his sons and his daughters. But David strengthened himself in the Lord his God.*"[2] (*1 Samuel 30:6*) "*But you, beloved, building yourselves up on your most holy faith, praying in the Holy Spirit.*"[3] (*Jude 1: 20*) God's Word tell us believers how we can strengthen and build ourselves up also. These Scriptures really helped me. I prayed in the Holy Spirit all the time. This enabled me to continue to pray and stand in the gap for my son. It is important to stay in God's word. This will help you when you are standing for something to be manifested. People will let you down, but God's Word will never fail. It will keep you going and help you stay encouraged.

CONTINUING TO SERVE THE LORD

Through all of this, God still allowed me to continue serving him. He trusted me to teach His Word and lead teams into prison ministry and rehabilitation centers. What an honor that although my own son was in and out of jail and addicted to drugs, I was able to go in and minister to others that were locked up. I couldn't believe it. God is so good. He does have a sense of humor. I knew that God was in all of this. It was not about me or my son, but about God's love and grace. He really loves us so very much!

"Although my own son was in and out of jail and addicted to drugs, I was able to go in and minister to others that were locked up."

AN ENCOURAGEMENT

While you are standing and waiting patiently for your children, grandchildren, or special loved one to be delivered, make sure you stay focused on the things of God. Serve and minister to others while you are waiting. Get involved with your church or a local outreach. This will help you to stay strong and focused on God. It will get our minds off ourselves and the pain we are going through. The Lord will direct you where to get involved. "*Trust in the Lord with all your heart, And lean not on your own understanding; In all your ways acknowledge Him, And He shall direct your paths.*" [4] (*Proverbs 3:5-6*)

STANDING ON GOD'S WORD

This is another verse that helped me realize I wasn't the only person going through something like this: "*Beloved, do not think it strange concerning the fiery trial which is to try you, as though some strange thing happened to you; but rejoice to the extent that you partake of Christ's sufferings, that when His glory is revealed, you may also be glad with exceeding joy.*" [5] (*1 Peter 4:12-13*)

NOTES/PRAYERS FOR LOVED ONES

Behold, I am the Lord, the God of all flesh. Is there anything too hard for Me?

Jeremiah 32:27

CHAPTER 8

FRIDAY NIGHT PRAYER

Zoe Christian Fellowship had such an impact on my life. We were taught the Word of God, and prayer went forth! Once a month we would have all-night prayer sessions, and on Friday nights, we would meet to pray in Compton. This was the Power House prayer group. Many were there whom the enemy had robbed, and we were taking back what belonged to us.

There is a men's rehabilitation home a few blocks away from Zoe Christian Fellowship called Catholic Rainbow Outreach (CRO). Pastor Ben Read presides over this ministry. They are born again, Spirit-filled Catholics. Every Sunday, they would come and fill up three or four rows with men from the home. I would pray and say, "Lord, I thank you. I see my son Travis also with these men; I see him sitting with them and worshiping you."

The Scriptures from His Word helped me see that nothing is impossible with God. So that's what I did, I prayed as if my son was totally set free from drugs and serving God. I could see him in church, praising and worshiping God, and teaching His word.

Although I couldn't see any changes yet with my eyes, I still had to stand and remain standing on God's Word and His promises. I saw the fulfillment of His promises with my heart of faith. As it is written, *'I have made you a father of many nations' in the presence of Him whom he believed - God, who gives life to the dead and calls those things which do not exist as though they did; who, contrary to hope, in hope believed, so that he became the father of many nations, according to what was spoken, 'So shall your descendants be.'"* [1] *(Romans 4:17–18).* These Scriptures were very encouraging to me. *"Therefore I say to you, whatever things you ask when you pray, believe that you receive them, and you will have them."* [2] *(Mark 11:24)*

I prayed these Scriptures continually and I still do today on any situation that might come up. It is God's Word that kept me strong through those 14 years that I had to stand and believe that my son would be set free from all addictions.

I had purposed in my mind to stay around strong uncompromising Christians. They were dedicated to pray for me and my son. They were there for me when things really got tough. I can't tell you enough how important it is to be around strong Christians who know how to pray. Thank God for intercessors.

THE UNEXPECTED

I remember once when my parents were on one of their vacations, they had asked me to take care of their home. No one was to be staying there at this time. I would get phone calls from the neighbors letting me know what was going on at my parent's house. I grew up in this neighborhood, and everyone would watch out for each other. When I drove up, I saw someone come out of the house. It was a woman. I found out her name was Karen. I didn't know her, but my son sure did. This was his new girlfriend. She and Travis had been staying in my parent's house while they were out of town. She was quite a few years older than my son. I also found out that more people were staying there as well. This didn't go over well with me. My parents didn't know any of this. I had everyone leave quickly.

Travis and Karen ended up staying together. My parents helped them get into a mobile trailer home only two blocks away from them. This wasn't a good situation. The Lord had blessed me with a new home as well, but it was across town.

AN UNEXPECTED BLESSING

One day my son called. He sounded very excited. He said, "Mom, I really need to talk to you." My door was closed for him to live with me, but my heart was still open. He told me I was going to be a grandmother. I was completely surprised. Karen was quite a few years older than Travis, so this was the last thing I was expecting to hear. I thought "This is just great. Both of them are on drugs and now a poor baby is thrown into this situation! Where does that leave this new sweet little baby?" I thank God for answered

"My door was closed for him to live with me, but my heart was still open."

prayer. Karen stopped using drugs the minute she found out she was pregnant, and the Lord continued to have His hand on my grandchild every step of the way. Every time I would see her I would say, "Can I lay hands on you and pray over you and the baby?" She would always say, "Yes, of course!" I would think, "Thank you, Jesus." We found out that the baby was a girl. I was so happy, because a child is truly of the Lord.

Now it was not God's perfect plan for Travis and Karen to be living together without being married, but oh, how He can turn things around for the good! My granddaughter was to be a part of His plan. God protected her from the very minute she was conceived. Her name was already chosen, and it was to be Sarah, which means Princess. She was, and still is today, a princess. Even though she wasn't yet born, God had a purpose for her. Once again, I had no idea where God was going with all of this, but He knew. Prayer was the key, and my intercessors stayed quite busy. Not only were these three lives about to change, but mine was to change as well.

"Even though she wasn't yet born, God had a purpose for her."

NOTES/PRAYERS FOR LOVED ONES

Behold, I am the Lord, the God of all flesh. Is there anything too hard for Me?
Jeremiah 32:27

CHAPTER 9

BECOMING MORE THAN A GRANDMA

On March 4, 1996, Sarah Katherine Cox was brought into this world. I started taking her to church when she was just seven days old. I would go by and pick her up. We went shopping a lot too. I gave my beautiful little granddaughter the nickname of "Pooh" and I still call her that today.

We were inseparable. She stayed with me often, and I loved it. My dad and mom were close to her as well. She was such a blessing to so many of us. I found myself taking her everywhere with me. I would take her with me when I had to teach at church. She was so good and would stay right with me. When it was time to take her back to the trailer where her parents lived, my heart would break. I had to trust God that He would take care of her. I prayed that angels would encamp around her and the trailer she lived in as well. There were so many strange people that would come and go out of that trailer. I continued to pray in the Holy Spirit and to trust the Lord.

CHANGING MY WAY OF PRAYING

I remember when the Holy Spirit directed me in another way to pray for my son and his new family. My granddaughter was almost two years old by now and I so desperately wanted her out of that atmosphere. I knew this was the Lord's will as well. "*But all things that are exposed are made manifest by the light, for whatever makes manifest is light.*" [1] (*Ephesians 5:13*) The things that are reproved will be 'exposed'

"It takes prayer and faith to move mountains, and nothing is too hard for God."

God wanted those things in my son's life that were done and kept in secret to be EXPOSED. I wanted the Lord to put a beacon light on them. I wanted the devil to be EXPOSED. God sees everything. I wanted my little granddaughter to be in a light-filled home. This mountain of darkness had to be removed. It takes prayer and faith to move mountains, and nothing is too hard for God. "*Behold, I am the Lord, the God of all flesh: Is there anything too hard for me?*" [2] (*Jeremiah 32:27*) I knew the answer was, "Of course not!"

ANOTHER PHONE CALL

I received a phone call from Karen one afternoon in February of 1998. She said the police had been there and their home had been raided. This took place only a few days after I changed my way of praying. A K-9 unit was brought in because God wanted everything exposed. They arrested Travis and others who were there as well.

Another couple had been living there with Travis and Karen, and they had a baby girl also.

Some would wonder why the police didn't take the babies that day. I knew this was God protecting my granddaughter once again. Karen knew that the police would return the very next day and bring Child Protective Services with them. She called me and asked, "Trenda, would you please come and get Sarah?" She had written a note giving me full custody of Sarah. Sarah was nearly two years old at this time. That note saved Sarah from going into the foster care system. God knew she was only to be with her family. The Lord had his hand on everything; that's why they didn't take her. Unfortunately, the other baby was placed in foster care.

"That note saved Sarah from going into the foster care system."

I thank the Lord that Karen wrote the note that day. She loved Sarah enough to give her to me; that must have been a very hard thing for her to do. I asked my dad to go and pick Sarah up for me. I was across town and was concerned that Child Protective Services would come back before I could get to her. Travis was back in jail again; Karen disappeared and no one knew where she had gone. The good thing was that I had Sarah with me. God's timing was perfect, but my life was about to change dramatically.

MORE CHANGES

All of a sudden, I was a full-time mom again. I had to raise Sarah. I had to wean her from the bottle, potty train her, and whatever else came along. I still ran my own business, and I was still teaching, now in the Evangelist Department. I had to make some major decisions. I prayed about it and felt the Lord wanting me to step down from teaching so I could focus on raising my granddaughter. He still allowed me to serve as an alter worker, because this was my heart. Raising Sarah was a big responsibility. She needed me to be there for her. My parents would help me, but I was fully responsible. The courts made me her guardian. Sarah never had to attend children's court. This was very unusual, but I knew it was God protecting her.

I was able to receive some financial help in raising Sarah. All of the money went towards her schooling and clothing. I had to place her in day care at our church. Later, when she was of school age, I enrolled her in a Christian elementary school. Travis and Karen had to pay this assistance money back to the state. They understood that it was due to the bad choices they had made.

MY ATTITUDE

My attitude grew indifferent towards Travis and Karen. I really didn't care where they were now. I was still praying for them, but my heart was not in it. I was so tired of the two of them. My parents had finally closed the door to them too.

Eight months had gone by, and Travis was still out there somewhere. We had no idea where he was living, and there was still no word from Karen either. I really didn't want to see either one of them. I knew this wasn't the right attitude to have, but I felt justified. Travis started coming by my mother's house at times, when I was there, to see Sarah. He was still using drugs, so I had to be very careful. One particular day when he was visiting, he heard Sarah call me Mommy, and that upset him so much. He said to me, "Remember, Mom, you are Grandma, not Mommy; she has one already." My attitude was still out of line, so I didn't answer Travis very respectfully. I had taken on the role of Sarah's mother, and I felt I should go all the way with this. The Lord had to remind me, through His Word, that I had closed the door, but not my heart. I had forgotten that my heart had to remain open.

THE SOCIAL WORKER

The social worker came to my home to make sure Sarah was being well taken care of and in a good place. She advised me to legally adopt Sarah. This would prevent Travis or Karen from ever taking her back into their custody. Given the circumstances of the situation, she felt I would have no problem adopting her. This made sense to me. All of a sudden, this verse rose up so big in my spirit, I responded and said to her, "No way! My God is able to turn this whole thing around." She told me I needed to realize that Travis and Karen were too old to change, that the damage had been done, and nothing was going to change for them. I told her, "But God is able to help them change. Nothing is too hard for God."

"Behold, I am the Lord, the God of all flesh: Is there anything too hard for me?" [2] *(Jeremiah 32:27)*

The social worker didn't want to hear any more, so she left. I knew God was faithful to His Word, but still thought to myself, "When is all of this going to change?" Guilt would often step in, and I felt bad for receiving the assistance check every month. I reminded myself that it was for Sarah. I did have a lot of financial responsibility, and I needed help with her schooling and clothing. It truly was a blessing.

NOTES/PRAYERS FOR LOVED ONES

Behold, I am the Lord, the God of all flesh. Is there anything too hard for Me?
Jeremiah 32:27

CHAPTER 10

READY FOR A REAL CHANGE

Time passed, Sarah was getting older, and things were starting to get a little easier for me. My business was steady and life was more manageable. Church was great. I had so much support from other brothers and sisters in the Lord. My parents were back on track with me. I continued praying for my son. I knew the devil still had a hold on him, but I also knew he had to let him go. I kept my love tough to keep him from trying to move back in with me.

MY SON WAS READY

On October 15, 1998, I received the phone call that I had been waiting years for. It was Travis telling me he was finally ready for help. He was 29 years old now and 14 years had passed since he started this journey into destruction. I had been standing in faith for so long that I found this hard to believe at first. Travis knew about the men's rehabilitation home that was nearby at Zoe Christian Fellowship. He asked me if I would pick him up and take him there. I told him, "No, you will have to find another way to get there." I gave him the phone number to Minister Elder Carter from Zoe. "Ask him to take you there if you want," I said. This was totally up to him. When a drug addict needs help, he has to really want it. Many times, drug addicts want others to help do what only they can do to change things for themselves. You can't interfere. You can't feel sorry for them and enable them. What you can do is pray. I know God is always ready to set people free, but they have to be ready to be set free. That day, Elder Carter picked my son up and took him to the rehabilitation home. This was the first time Travis wanted to do things God's way. There were other times he attempted to get clean when he was in jail. I needed to see if he was serious and how long this would last.

The Lord reminded me of all my prayers and the many years of confessing His Word over Travis, "*God calls those things that do not exist as though they did.*" [1] (*Romans 4:17*). All those times, I would envision him sitting in the church with the other men. And now, here he was 14 years later, sitting right there with those men in the pews, worshiping God in a way I had never seen him do before. He seemed so sincere and so in love with Jesus.

"All those times, I would envision him sitting in the church with the other men."

Things seemed to go well enough that Sarah began visiting her daddy on Sundays and any day he was free. I would take her to the men's home to visit, and she loved it. The other men in the home were good men, but being the protective grandma that I was, I made sure she was never left alone or out of my sight. I noticed Travis was being very protective of Sarah now as well. He was so careful with her. They were always close to each other, but now they became really close. I couldn't believe the change I saw in him. The pastor said Travis was a true leader. He had the respect of the other men in the home as well. I knew Travis was a leader, and the Lord had a plan for him. It was amazing to see the grace and mercy the Lord poured over Travis. His mind should have been so messed up by all the drugs he did. In reality, he should not even be alive. He is a walking miracle. God did the incredible. The pastor and his wife loved Travis. They still keep in touch with each other to this day.

ONE MORE PHONE CALL

As unexpected as the call I received from Travis was, I got another phone call from him. This time he called to say he had heard from Karen. This had to be God. He said she was ready to get help. She wanted to get into a women's home, and Travis and his pastor were able to find her one. She went in on May 29, 1999. My attitude was not very nice, and that came across on the phone to Travis. I knew it wasn't right. My heart was so hard towards Karen. The Holy Spirit knew it. Now, if I wanted to be blessed, I had to change my attitude and my heart. So I asked God to help.

My son told me she got saved and became filled with the Holy Spirit. My answer was, "So that's nice," I sounded very sarcastic and not very faith-filled. You have to realize that Karen had not seen Sarah for nearly two years, and I felt she had abandoned her. If I was honest with myself, I was very angry about this. Thank God He doesn't keep track of all our sins. My attitude needed adjusting, as did my heart. I needed to remember all that Jesus had delivered me from and all He had done for me.

One day Karen called me to ask if she could see Sarah. I blurted out harshly to her, "And how do you plan on doing that?" Karen lived in a rehabilitation home that was over an hour and a half away, and she had no car. She told me she could take the bus. She also said it might take her several hours because she had to transfer to three buses before she could get there. I told her it would be okay, but I heard in my spirit "Go pick her up". I said aloud, "What"? Again I heard "Go pick her up". This time I listened, and I went and picked her up. We went to a local park so Karen could play with Sarah for awhile. This was very difficult for me as I was still resentful towards Karen. This was also very hard for Karen. The Holy Spirit impressed upon me that it took a lot for her to make that phone call. I had to get through all of this with God's strength and help. I knew God could turn things around if I let Him.

We actually had a wonderful day. Karen and I created a bond that day. Sarah and I went to the women's home several times after that to visit her mommy. Karen even met me at court a few times. I had to go to court often, but Sarah never went; she stayed with my mom on those days. What a blessing that she never had to be brought into court.

Karen changed right before my very eyes. She was so in love with Jesus, and she was still in love with my son. She became a true student of God's Word and stayed focused on her recovery and on her growth in the Lord. Wanting to honor God, both Karen and Travis made a decision to abstain from sexual relations until they were married. This became a two and a half year wait. God blessed them for this decision.

"Wanting to honor God, both Karen and Travis made a decision to abstain from sexual relations until they were married."

Not long after this, I brought Karen on board to work with me in my cleaning business, and I later promoted her to Assistant Manager. She has been with me at Trenda's Cleaning Service for the past 12 years now. She is such a blessing to me.

GOD WAS PREPARING ME

Shortly after Travis was in the men's home, God directed me to take Sarah to a wonderful church called Cottonwood Church in Los Alamitos, California. Bayless Conley is the Senior Pastor. After ten years of serving the Lord at Zoe Christian Fellowship, I felt the Lord leading me to attend Cottonwood regularly. I couldn't understand it at first. I talked with Pastor Ed about it, and he encouraged me to be obedient to the leading of the Holy Spirit. I really didn't want to leave Zoe. Pastor Ed knew I would be going to a great teaching church. Pastor Ed and Pastor Bayless were friends. Pastor Ed had ministered at Cottonwood and Pastor Bayless had come to speak at Zoe as well. This change of churches didn't seem to make sense to me. I had prayed for so long for Travis to surrender to the Lord. Now he was attending Zoe, and the Lord was directing me to leave Zoe and serve Him at Cottonwood. I really had no idea where God was going with all this.

OCTOBER 1999, GRADUATION FOR TRAVIS

Finally graduation day was here. Travis was graduating from the men's home, and my parents were able to witness all of this and see their prayers being answered. Close friends and members of Zoe were there to celebrate with us as well. We all witnessed the miracle of our prayers being manifested. I was one happy mom. There was a flood of tears of joy.

After graduation, Travis stayed at the men's home until June 2000. He was finally ready to live drug-free. Travis found a job and was working to support himself. I allowed him to stay with me for a short period of time. He was with me about two months when he said to me, "Mom, your list of rules is longer than the one in the men's home", and he moved out and into his own apartment. He was living a sober, productive life now. God is so good and so faithful to His Word. Thank you, Lord Jesus.

THE BIG WEDDING DAY

On March 10, 2001, Travis and Karen were married. The wedding was held at Zoe Christian Fellowship in Whittier, California. Elder Carter married them, the same Elder Carter who had taken Travis to the men's home just three years before. It was such a joyous wedding. Sarah was five years old and the perfect little flower girl. This was a day filled with rejoicing. We had so much to be thankful for. There were tears everywhere, but happy ones, of course. God deserved all the glory and honor. He is so good; I keep repeating this because He truly is! I had waited a long time to see this day come. It was finally here and was like an incredible dream come true.

I still had custody of Sarah at this time because we had one more court date to fulfill. She was with her mom and dad most of the time by now, but we still needed to do things the proper legal way.

A SURPRISE BLESSING FOR ME

I was 53 years old now, going to a new church and starting a new chapter in my life. I had been attending Cottonwood Church for almost a year at this time. God was working behind the scenes to set up something incredible for me. I had no idea that he was preparing me for my husband.

NOTES/PRAYERS FOR LOVED ONES

Behold, I am the Lord, the God of all flesh. Is there anything too hard for Me?
Jeremiah 32:27

CHAPTER 11

HAPPILY EVER AFTER FOR ALL

In December 2001, I started dating a wonderful man named Ed Lineback, Jr. We quickly fell in love. Ed asked permission from Travis if he could marry me, and my son whole-heartedly agreed, as long as we went to marriage counseling. We went through marriage counseling at Cottonwood Church. It was an eight-week course, and it was fantastic. We still use some of the tools we learned in that course after 12 years of marriage. My best friend said it was like God just dropped Ed down into the family. I had been single for 27 years when God wanted to bless me with a wonderful husband. God is so good. My Ed was just waiting for me. This wonderful man had never been married before and had no extra baggage to bring into our marriage. God does bless exceedingly abundantly beyond all we could ever ask or imagine!

OUR LAST DAY IN COURT

What a blessing it was to finally have one last day in court! We just couldn't believe it. This was such a great ending to our story that even the judge commented on it. He said that things usually don't turn out this way. The parents don't typically stay together and they rarely comply with the court orders. But both Travis and Karen fulfilled all of the requirements. Travis had a good job, an apartment, and even a car. He had been clean and sober for nearly three years, and for Karen, it had been two years. The judge asked me if I wanted to say anything, and I said, "Yes, I am getting married!" The whole court clapped for us. I never could have imagined the way our lives would turn out. God is so good.

OUR BIG DAY

Ed and I were married on June 22, 2002, and Travis walked me down the aisle. There were so many tears of joy as my parents were able to be there to celebrate with us. Pastor Ed Smith and all of Zoe Christian Fellowship made such an incredible impact on all of our lives personally. I truly believe that if it wasn't for this ministry; the teaching, the all-night prayer sessions, the dedicated intercessors, and all the other resources that were available to us, we would not be where we are today. It is a good feeling to know that God is directing you, especially as you leave one ministry to go to another, with the support and love from your prior church. I am forever grateful to Pastor Ed and all of our brothers and sisters in Christ who were always there for us and gave us unconditional love.

THE MOVE TO COTTONWOOD CHURCH

Cottonwood was just starting a new ministry called Celebrate Recovery. Travis and Karen knew that was where God was calling them to serve. They wanted to help others who were struggling as they'd once struggled. God called both of them to serve the Lord and what better way than through a recovery program.

What a blessing! I listen to my son teach from Celebrate Recovery podcasts; it still amazes me every time. On October 15, 2013, Travis celebrated 15 years of being clean and sober. God is so wonderful. He is amazing. I love Him so much!

NEVER AN ENDING, ALWAYS A NEW BEGINNING

This story is not over. It's only the beginning of a new chapter in all our lives. God's Word is true, and nothing is ever too hard for Him. God hasn't forgotten you or your children; He hears your prayers. Never give up. When you close the door, you're not closing your heart. The Lord will give you the strength and the wisdom you need to go through anything. He loves you dearly.

"God's Word is true, and nothing is ever too hard for Him."

"The Lord shall increase you more and more, you and your children."[1] (Psalms 115:14)

God's *Love* never fails

With God *All* things are possible

NOTES/PRAYERS FOR LOVED ONES

Behold, I am the Lord, the God of all flesh. Is there anything too hard for Me?
Jeremiah 32:27

SALVATION PRAYER

Do you know Jesus as your Savior? Would you like to make things right with God? Pray this simple prayer aloud:

"Lord Jesus, I thank you that you loved me so much that you died on the cross to set me free from sin. I confess with my mouth that Jesus is Lord. I believe in my heart that you rose from the dead and live forever so that I might live forever, too. Come into my heart, cleanse me of all sin and be the Lord of my life. I thank you for saving me. I believe that I am not the same."

According to God's Word, *"If you confess with your mouth the Lord Jesus and believe in your heart that God has raised Him from the dead, you will be saved. For with the heart one believes unto righteousness, and with the mouth confession is made unto salvation."* [1] (*Romans 10:9-10*) If you just prayed that prayer of faith, my friend, you are truly born again because God's Word says so. Don't allow anyone or any thought to tell you differently. God cannot lie. You are saved and Jesus lives in you right now and always will. Welcome to the Kingdom of God, my precious friend.

THE BAPTISM OF THE HOLY SPIRIT

In God's Word Jesus says to ask and you shall receive. Just like salvation, the baptism of the Holy Spirit is also free. Ask and you shall receive. It is that simple. "*Nevertheless I tell you the truth. It is to your advantage that I go away; for if I do not go away, the Helper will not come to you; but if I depart, I will send Him to you.*" [1] (*John 16: 7*) "*Behold, I send the Promise of My Father upon you; but tarry in the city of Jerusalem until you are endued with with power on high.*" [2] (*Luke 24:49*)

There were so many times I did not know how to pray for my son or what to do next. When I received the baptism of the Holy Spirit it was the extra help that I really needed. "*Likewise the Spirit also helps in our weaknesses. For we do not know what we should pray for as we ought, but the Spirit Himself makes intercession for us with groanings which cannot be uttered. Now He who searches the hearts knows what the mind of the Spirit is, because he makes intercession for the saints according to the will of God.*" [3] (*Romans 8:26-27*) According to God's Word, when we pray in our heavenly language, we are speaking directly to God, not to man. Remember, Satan cannot interpret God's spirit. "*For he that speaketh in an unknown tongue speaketh not unto men, but unto God: for no man understandeth him; howbeit in the spirit he speaketh mysteries.*" [4] (*1 Corinthians 14:2 KJV*) Also according to God's Word, praying in the spirit (other tongues) helps build us up. We need to be built up so we can face anything.

"But you, beloved, building yourselves up on your most holy faith; praying in the Holy Spirit" [5] (*Jude 1:20a NASB*) *"So I say to you, ask, and it will be given to you; seek, and you find; knock, and it will be opened to you. For everyone who asks receives, and he who seeks finds, and to him who knocks it will be opened. If a son asks for bread from any father among you, will he give him a stone? Or if he asks for a fish, will he give him a serpent instead of a fish? Or if he asks for an egg, will he offer him a scorpion? If you then, being evil, know how to give good gifts to your children, how much more will your heavenly Father give the Holy Spirit to those who ask Him!"* [6] (*Luke 11: 9-13*) *"And they were all filled with the Holy Spirit and began to speak with other tongues, as the Spirit gave them utterance."* [7] (*Acts 2:4*) Jesus says ask and you shall receive. For everyone who asks receives, so enjoy the benefits of the baptism of the Holy Spirit.

END NOTES

INTRODUCTION

1. Jeremiah 31:15
2. Jeremiah 32:27

CHAPTER 2

1. Isaiah 59:16

CHAPTER 3

1. John 10:10
2. Romans 10:13

CHAPTER 4

1. Acts 1:8
2. John 14:16-17
3. Romans 8:26
4. Genesis 12:3
5. John 10:10 (NIV)
6. Ephesians 6:13 (KJV)
7. Matthew 19:26
8. Hebrews 12:1

CHAPTER 7

1. Philippians 4:13
2. 1 Samuel 30:6
3. Jude 1:20
4. Proverbs 3:5-6
5. 1 Peter 4:12-13

CHAPTER 8

1. Romans 4:17-18
2. Mark 11:24

CHAPTER 9

1. Ephesians 5:13
2. Jeremiah 32:27

CHAPTER 10

1. Romans 4:17

CHAPTER 11

1. Psalms 115:14

SALVATION PRAYER

1. Romans 10:9-10

BAPTISM OF HOLY SPIRIT

1. John 16:7
2. Luke 24:49
3. Romans 8:26-27
4. I Corinthians 14:2 (KJV)
5. Jude 1:20a (NASB)
6. Luke 11:9-13
7. Acts 2:4

Made in the USA
Middletown, DE
16 May 2018